The little book of
BIG INTENTIONS

Guidance for embodied, purposeful living

Erin Lee

INVOCATION

May you BE
all that you intend

CONTENTS

TRUTH	9
COMPASSION	15
BALANCE	19
GRACE	25
SOVEREIGNTY	29
GRATITUDE	35
SURRENDER	41
PRESENCE	47
WISDOM	53
LOVE	59
ACCEPTANCE	65
FORGIVENESS	71
CLARITY	77
PLAY	81
CONNECTION	87
POWER	93
TRUST	97
RECEPTIVITY	101
COURAGE	107
PATIENCE	113
HUMILITY	119
SERVICE	125
BLISS	129
KINDNESS	135
CURIOSITY	139
PEACE	145
REFLECTION	151

GETTING INTENTIONAL

When we choose to live with intention, we move
through life with *purpose* and *meaning*.

As long as you've got your body and your breath, you have
the power *within you* to activate intended experiences.

In Sanskrit (the root language of yoga) intention is known as

SANKALPA

... meaning a vow that aligns with our highest truth.

When you set an intention,
you're speaking the language of your soul.

Sometimes we lose touch with what feels meaningful,
and a sense of *disconnection* sets in.

Getting intentional is a conscious decision
– a *resolve* that realigns us with our true nature.

Listening to our soul's deepest aspirations awakens the heart.

We become **inspired** again.

Vital life force flows back in.

inspired = in-spirit

From a whole spirited place, we navigate our way through
life on purpose and soul-FULL.

A greater sense of *connection* to life around us,
and within us, is the ultimate result.

EMBODYING INTENTION

In yoga, the physical poses – asanas, are just one aspect of the practice. Yet it's in the *physical* body where we get to *feel* intention at a cellular level.

Beginning with a vow of **mind and heart,** we amplify our intention through the breath. The breath is the gateway between the mind and the body – the intention gets **felt** through the *presence* of the body.

Energy flows where awareness goes.

Practising intention embodiment on the yoga mat helps the effects ripple out into everyday life **off the yoga mat,** supporting us to move through life's pleasant *and* unpleasant times with more awareness, resilience and capacity for skilful action.

It doesn't matter whether you practise yoga or not: every BODY has the opportunity to
embody
the power of intention.

EM·BODI·MENT
= *we are **meant** to be **in** our body*

USING THE YOGA IMAGES

This isn't about trying to look exactly like the figures in the images or any-BODY else for that matter.

The images depicting each yoga pose, are meant as a guide only to show you an expression of the pose.

What's **really** important when you're using the images and guidance is that you
stay present along the journey toward the pose,
honouring any physical issues you're currently managing.

This is a compassionate, non-harmful way to move through life.

CHOOSING AN INTENTION

You can start at the beginning and work in a linear way
through each intention.

OR

You can allow yourself to intuitively source an intention.

Take a few deep breaths, open your heart, and
be guided.

Once you have selected an intention:

REFLECT

How does the intention and image make you feel?

What is the first message that lands for you?

Only YOU will know the relevance this intention has in your life right now.

EMBODY

- Contemplate the words about the intention.
- Read the guidance on how to come into the yoga pose.
- Come into the posture, and embody the intention.

ALLOW

Once you're in the yoga pose, *just breathe.*
The breath is the bridge, journeying the intention from your mind into your physical body.

TRUTH

When we are searching for Truth, what we're *really* doing
is journeying beyond the limits of our human experience.

Truth lives in your eternal soul.

However, along the human journey, we can mistake Truth
for opinions, preferences, perspectives and judgements.

We can also fall into the trap of trying to *think* our way to
the Truth, by weighing up the pros and cons of a situation.

Sometimes our emotions try to hijack us,
and have us believe that *they* are the Truth.

Truth doesn't live 'out there' — somewhere outside of us.
Nor does it live in some kind of temporary experience,
like a thought or emotion.

Truth lives in your ever-lasting soul,
waiting to be unveiled and realised.

There's nothing more to *add on* to *awaken* Truth ...

Truth is realised through a process of subtraction
– we must **un-know** what we *think* the Truth is.

In doing so, we allow human obstacles to dissolve into a
larger field of conscious awareness,
where all possibility lives – including Truth.

From a space of 'not-knowing',
Truth can be *felt* – and realised.

Your Truth is an expression of your soul, otherwise referred to as your *true nature*.

EMBODYING TRUTH

Tadasana
MOUNTAIN POSE

Mountain Pose asks you to stand tall in your own Truth, keeping your heart open with an understanding that temporary conditions will pass.

☼ This is an invitation for you to awaken Truth in your body.

- From a standing position, bring your big toes together, and slightly separate the heels.

- Keep a microbend in your knees, and imagine roots branching from your feet, down into the core of the Earth.

- Extend your arms long by your sides. With the palms facing forward, reach out through all your fingers.

- Rotate the thighs in toward one another, then broaden across the front of the pelvis.

- Activate the core by engaging the pelvic floor, and drawing the front ribs in toward one another.

- Breathe in as you lengthen through your side waists.

- Breathe out to relax your shoulders, drawing the chin in toward your throat. Feel the crown of your head rise up toward the sky, resembling the peak of a mountain.

- Close your eyes or keep the gaze soft, as you allow the breeze of your breath to journey through your inner landscape.

Invite Truth in.

COMPASSION

There is good reason to intend more Compassion right now ...

Whether it's for the suffering of the world at large, or for discomfort and pain unfolding in your own life, *awakening* your Compassionate heart is the way forward.

It's a *radical act* requiring **courage** to rise above your own primal survival tendencies, rooted in fear.

If you are experiencing pain right now, it's only human to feel mentally or emotionally consumed by it ...
If you are witnessing someone else's pain, you might find yourself wanting to look away ...

What's courageous though is to welcome the suffering into your heart. Allow it to be held there with tenderness, and with *acceptance.* Suffering is something we all experience. When we realise this, we awaken Compassion.

Be mindful of the tendency to want to fix or change the suffering. It's not that it won't change – everything does.

The only way to ease tension and move through suffering, is to first bring it into your heart.

It's from the heart that the greatest pain has the potential to be transformed, through **love in action.**

EMBODYING COMPASSION

Sukhasana
EASY POSE

The Tibetan Buddhist practice of Tonglen meditation (otherwise known as the practice of 'sending and taking') brings suffering into the heart – the very place where suffering can be liberated.

✺ This is an invitation for you to awaken Compassion in your body.

- Sit comfortably with your legs crossed, ensuring your hips are positioned a little higher than your knees (use a cushion to sit on if necessary).

- Close your eyes *or* keep them open with a soft gaze.

- Take a few full breaths in and out. Lengthen the spine and awaken the torso on the inhalation. Relax any unnecessary physical tension on the exhalation.

- Now bring to mind someone who is experiencing suffering. It might be you, yourself, who is going through a difficult time or experiencing pain. Or someone or something else.

- On your next inhale, bring the suffering into your heart as if you're saying 'yes' to it.

- Feel your heart softening as you breathe out.

- Inhale and bring the suffering into your heart, allowing it to be alchemised into a sense of care.

- Exhale and breathe out with Compassion.

- Breathe in, taking in the pain, the discomfort, the unpleasantness ...

- Breath out for relief, peace, healing and wellbeing.

Invite Compassion in.

BALANCE

The natural world continually ebbs and flows, creates and destroys, rises and falls, expands and contracts – it's forever seeking equilibrium.

You are a part of nature too.
As an Earth-ling, you are automatically alchemising as you navigate your way through life, finding Balance.

Sometimes, the greatest lessons in Balance come through the hard knocks that send us flying afar ...

Small knocks endured over a long period of time, can also leave us feeling misaligned.

What can we do when we're feeling like this?

There's no better guru to turn to than Mother Nature.

Notice how she deals with a tree that falls in the forest ...
There might be a temporary shock, but watch how new growth emerges in the space created from the change.

See how it takes *time* and *appropriate conditions* for plants to grow, flowers to blossom and coral reefs to spawn.

We can't force nature to hurry up her processes.

What we *can* do is love and nurture her along the way, supporting her to flourish in her own time.

To return to Balance,
get intimate with nature.

Know what being off-Balance feels like in
your body, energy and mind.

Tend to these areas as if you were tending to a zen garden –
with patience, care and presence.

Feel how you and Mother Nature are the same.

Remember how connected you both are and you will
be *shown* the way back to Balance.

EMBODYING BALANCE

Vrksasana
TREE POSE

In the same way that a tree stands firm but remains flexible
in changing weather, Tree Pose asks that we deepen our
connection to Earth, while remaining flexible
to manage the sways and swaggers of life.

☀ **This is an invitation for you to restore Balance in your body.**

- From a standing position, gaze at a focal point ahead. Press one foot into the ground, keeping a microbend through the knee and activating the glutes.

- Gradually lift the other foot away from the ground, placing the sole against the inside of the calf or thigh of the standing leg. Angle the bent knee to the side.

- Root down through the standing foot as you raise your arms up toward the sky to resemble the long and flexible branches of a tree.

- Set your fingers in Gyan Mudra to promote focus and wisdom. Connect your thumbs with your forefingers and extend the last three fingers long.

- As you breathe in, broaden across your heartspace, relaxing your shoulders away from your ears.

- Breathe out and point the base of your spine down toward the Earth, keeping your pelvis neutral.

- Lift the crown of your head high toward the vast sky above, matching this effort with your deep connection to Earth beneath you.

Invite Balance in.

GRACE

In Yoga Sutra 2.46, Patanjali refers to *sthira sukham asanam*, which translates to a 'stable and comfortable posture'. To achieve this in a yoga pose we must take *steady action* – consistent effort over time *without* unnecessary tension.

This how Grace works in everyday life.

Grace lives in the space that exists between effort and effortlessness.

Grace is the divine space *in* and *between* all things.

It's the music that happens in-between the notes
... the pause between impulse and response.
Grace is born in the balance of
action and non-action,
effort and ease.

Whatever position you find yourself in,
make sure there is space to allow the *God energy* of Grace
to move through you.

When we bring the stillness of our *being* into what we are *doing*, we tap into the miraculous flow of Grace.

EMBODYING GRACE

Natarajasana
DANCER'S POSE

To achieve balance in Dancer's Pose, take each step forward with steadiness **and** ease. Discover the Grace that lives in the space between effort and ease.

This is an invitation for you to notice Grace in your body.

- From a standing position, gaze gently at a single focal point ahead.

- Press the whole of your right foot firmly into the ground. Keep a microbend through the knee of that same leg, and activate the glutes.

- Begin to lift your left foot away from the ground, sending the heel toward your bottom. Catch the foot with your left hand and cup the inner arch with your fingers.

- Level both hips evenly. Broaden the tips of the collarbone.

- Lift through the crown of your head, and reach the right arm out ahead of you with your hand in Gyan Mudra to promote focus and wisdom as you prepare to expand – connect your thumb with your forefinger and extend the last three fingers long.

- Breathe in and begin pushing the left foot into your left hand. Breathe out to lean forward gradually, to your extent of this pose in this moment.

- Make sure you can still breathe.

Invite Grace in.

SOVEREIGNTY

Sovereignty is an old word, conjuring up archetypes of kings and queens living in kingdoms and castles.

We are also sovereign beings.

What creates Sovereignty is our personal *boundaries* – the borders of our values and free will.

Boundaries are a rudder for our soul, as we navigate the choices of life.

They keep us aligned with what feels most important.

With Sovereignty, we willingly stand up for what's most important to the core of our being.

If you've spent your life people-pleasing and worrying about what others think, speaking up about what FEELS right for you may be daunting ...

However being clear with others is an expression of *kindness,* and an act of love – for self and others.
Being unclear causes confusion and misunderstandings.

Freely express the needs of your inner world to the outer world. With your soul as your compass, speak up and reclaim the lay of your land.

What are the values you want to live by?

What scenarios no longer feel in alignment with your values?

Beyond old ingrained habits and egoic patterns lives your soul's truth. Dig deep now, and send love across your words and actions as you communicate your boundaries.

Always express boundaries with love.

EMBODYING SOVEREIGNTY

Virabhadrasana II
WARRIOR II POSE

In Warrior II Pose, we align from the ground up, *then* centre out. Moving through life connected to our values helps us express our boundaries with love.

✳ This is an invitation for you to reclaim Sovereignty in your body.

- From a standing position take a large step backwards with one foot, planting it down on an approximate 45-degree angle, toes pointing outwards.

- Bend through the front knee, looking down to check that it aligns with the middle toes (rather than the big toe).

- Align your front heel with the arch of your back foot. Imagine magnets are positioned on either heel — feel them being drawn toward one another, stabilising the legs to stand strong.

- Extend both arms out sideways — wrists in line with the shoulders, fingers outstretched and palms facing down. Send your focused, yet peaceful gaze across the middle finger of the front hand.

- Relax the jaw and shoulders, and broaden across the heartspace.

- Breathe in to lengthen through the side waists.

- Breathe out to activate the core — engage the pelvic floor and draw the front lower ribs in toward one another.

- Stand here with the certainty of a warrior, while keeping the heartspace peacefully open.

Invite Sovereignty in.

GRATITUDE

One day I sat down to get clear on what my big visions and
goals were for the year ahead ...

As I contemplated what to call in, I realised my life
already contained so many fulfilling experiences.

Sure, I could have added more money and other trinkets
to my list, yet what more would that give me on a *soul level*
if I was already experiencing my highest intentions?

Instead of writing down new goals,
I began *giving thanks* for the love, abundance and peace
I was already experiencing.

From that day forward, more experiences of love,
abundance and peace flooded my way, expanding beyond
any goal-setting strategy I'd previously tried.

Love grew.

Money appeared in the most unexpected ways,
and I always seemed to have enough.

I found more space and peace in between all the doing.

Life felt more in-flow – in soul alignment.

Gratitude is the fuel that
fills the heart and activates the soul.

Wishing for something more, *without* acknowledging and giving thanks for what you already have, is like trying to pour water into a cup that's already full.

When is enough *enough*?

Honour what's already in your cup.

Gratitude is the bridge that connects us
to the jet stream of our highest intentions.

EMBODYING GRATITUDE

Setu Bandhasana
BRIDGE POSE

Bridge Pose is a backbend that supports us to open our heart in Gratitude. An open heart is a receptive heart.

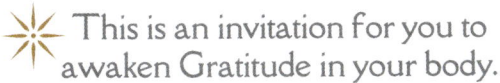 This is an invitation for you to awaken Gratitude in your body.

- Begin by lying on your back, knees bent with your feet flat on the ground.

- Place your arms on the ground alongside your body, palms facing down.

- Keep your head in line with the spine (without looking sideways). Now, press the feet and palms down into the Earth and lift your bottom away from it, sending your hips and heart up toward the sky.

- Walk your arms underneath your body, interlace your fingers and press the arms and shoulder blades into the Earth, expanding your heartspace.

- Breathe in deeply as you continue to say *YES* to everything that is here right now ...

- Stay here as you breathe out, allowing any unnecessary tension to dissolve.

Invite Gratitude in.

SURRENDER

Surrender is *a conscious decision to soften* resistance.

When we Surrender, we release the need to hold on or attach to anything — instead, we *allow* life to *BE*.

An exercise:

Clench your fists as tightly as you can.
Take a moment to experience what it *feels* like to hold on ...

Now, *release the grip* and relax your hands.

This is what it feels like to let go;
to Surrender.

We're not as in control of life as we *think* we are.
We can only keep our fists clenched for so long before harm is caused OR we completely exhaust ourselves from all the 'holding on'.

At some point, we *have* to loosen the grip.

Relinquishing control and surrendering
isn't about giving up ...

Surrender understands that a greater intelligence
keeps a natural order around life.

A prayer:

'Universe, I now release my resistance and invite you to show me the way from here.
I know and trust that you have my highest potential at heart.'

Loosen your grip and allow yourself to *be held by life.*

Notice how everything naturally falls back into place.

EMBODYING SURRENDER

Balasana
CHILD'S POSE

As a grounding pose, Child's Pose invites you to release 'the grip' and Surrender your heart to what exists here and now.

This is an invitation for you to Surrender your body.

- Place your hands and knees on the ground.

- Widen your knees, connect the big toes (untuck them) and send your sit bones back onto your heels. If there's a gap between your sit bones and heels, slip a cushion in the gap to support you to rest easier.

- Reach your hands as far forward as you can, palms facing down, forehead resting to the Earth. A cushion can also be placed under the forehead.

- Breathe in, feeling the expansion in your back body ...

- Breathe out through an open mouth, feeling your front body soften.

- Imagine each inhale is like a chimney sweep, collecting all that you're holding onto. Allow each exhale to relax any gripping sensations in the body, and release what you no longer need to hold onto.

- You might notice your mind also releasing its grip, surrendering the awareness back into a broader, more spacious field.

Invite Surrender in.

PRESENCE

When we offer our Presence,
life showers us with abundance.

Ordinary moments become extraordinary.
We awaken to parts of life we never knew existed.

In the newness of this moment, there's so much to
notice when the lens of our awareness is free
from bias and judgement.

With Presence, we watch moments unfold with a sense of
wonder and curiosity, as if it's our first time experiencing it –
no matter how many times we've experienced it.

Presence *connects* us to the fullness of life
that exists in each moment.

Without Presence, our attention drifts off in all sorts of
directions, like a boat that has separated from its anchor.
The body remains here, anchored to the present moment,
yet our mind has drifted someplace else.

This separation of body and mind creates a gap in our spirit
- we experience disconnection. The gap gives rise to fear,
presenting as worry and anxiety because there's nothing
keeping us grounded.

We grieve the separation, sensing something is missing.
We've lost our way.

In these moments, we need something
to tow the boat back to its anchor point.

We need to bring awareness back to the body.

As long as you have a body – and you're alive, you're
already armed with the perfect connector: **your breath**.

Invite the breath into the mind-body gap,
and fill up with Presence again.

The breath tethers our mind to our body,
as we bring awareness to the *felt sensations*
of each breath within the physical body.

Awareness travels along the breath, flooding every cell with
a sense of grounding and connection.

With our spirit whole again, we emanate Presence.

Remember what is already here.

EMBODYING PRESENCE

Dandasana
STAFF POSE

Staff Pose shows us how to remain here –
in this exact moment, despite any impulse we may have
to be someplace else.

✷ This is an invitation for you to awaken Presence in your body.

- Take a seat, extending your legs out in front of you.

- Shift the flesh of your buttocks away from the sit bones, ensuring a solid grounding. If needed, slip a cushion under your sit bones to ensure your hips are level with or higher than your knees.

- Draw your toes back towards your body, then press the backs of your heels down into the Earth, engaging your thigh muscles.

- Place your palms flat on the ground beside your hips. Lower your shoulders away from the ears.

- Tuck the chin in toward your throat, and lift the crown of your head toward the sky.

- Breathe in, sensing space between each vertebrae, all the way from your tailbone to the top of your spine.

- Breathe out, pressing down through your seat and rising up through the crown of your head.

- Rest your gaze on a single object ahead of you, with a sense of wonder and curiosity. In the background of your awareness, feel the breath flowing in and out of your body.

Invite Presence in.

WISDOM

Wisdom lives beyond the thinking mind.
It's the part of you that innately and intuitively
knows the higher road to take.

While you can develop Wisdom with experience and
increased understanding, it's not something you can learn by
becoming more intelligent. Wisdom must be unveiled.

You are born with Wisdom.

Wisdom is the lighthouse for your soul, shining
the way along higher roads that point to truth.

The road may get bumpy at times, yet Wisdom always leads
you to your soul – your highest potential
with outcomes that are universally beneficial.

Sometimes, when stormy weather sets in, it can be harder to
see the light. We may try other routes instead.

Our automatic stress response – including the whirlwind
of thoughts and emotions that come with it, clouds over our
'better judgement'. The higher road fogs over, as louder
energies like anger and fear lure us down another route.

We may even blindly follow *someone else's* Wisdom
when our own isn't so accessible.

At the crossroad of choices, Wisdom *discerns*.

Pause before taking the next step,
look beyond the changeable weather and
feel the certainty of the path of truth.

Be still and listen ...

hear the Wisdom of your heart.

EMBODYING WISDOM

Adho Mukha Svanasana
DOWNWARD FACING DOG

Downward Facing Dog invites us to drop the thinking mind and FEEL the body, bearing witness to ever-changing sensations and discerning the next step with 'right judgement'.

☼ This is an invitation for you to unveil Wisdom in your body.

- Place your hands and knees on the ground.

- Walk your hands a little further forward. Spread all your fingers wide, pressing the palms and underside of all knuckles into the Earth.

- Now, tuck your toes and lift your hips up toward the sky.

- Glance forward to check the hands are shoulder-width apart. Then, look back to check the feet are hip-width apart.

- Keep looking back now, gazing between your thighs or up towards your navel, keeping your ears in line with your biceps.

- Keep a bend through the knees, as you turn your inner thighs towards the space behind you.

- Now, send your heels toward the ground (they may not touch the ground, and that's okay).

- Draw your shoulders away from the ears, broaden the tips of your collarbone, and relax your neck.

- Find a rhythmic pace with your inhalations and exhalations as you lean your heart towards the thighs.

Invite Wisdom in.

LOVE

When Love flows freely, we feel at ease.
Without the medicine of Love,
we become sick – in a state of 'dis-ease'.

Obstacles to Love are often borne out of our past experiences.
We've felt Love come and go, sometimes involving
heartbreak. We may have told ourselves that we'll never trust
Love again. We may have withheld Love, in fear
of it not be acknowledged or returned.

As a result, we put *conditions* on Love.

It's easy to Love when convenient, but when things aren't
going our way obstacles like fear, judgement and aversion can
distort Love's presence.

Deep within us, we all desire unconditional Love.

Love is more than just a temporary emotion
or a one-off loving gesture ...

Unconditional Love holds everything, everyone, every view,
every opinion and every way of life in the same loving space.

You can even extend Love out,
while at the same time saying 'no'!

For true Love to flow,
we must give and receive

freely

without putting any rules in place.

EVERY person on this planet needs Love.
To give and take Love is the *perfect medicine*
– no prescription needed.

Notice how Love continues to flow
when she's free.

EMBODYING LOVE

Anjaneyasana
CRESCENT MOON POSE

Crescent Moon Pose encourages us to put in as much effort, as ease. It's in the middle of the two that Love flows through.

> ☀ This is an invitation for you to
> return to Love in your body.

- From a standing position take a large step backwards with one foot, staying on the ball of the back foot. For a modified version, drop your knee to the ground (see illustration).

- Frame your front foot with your hands. Keeping your front knee stacked over the ankle, breathe in to lift your arms up toward the sky. Keep your biceps in line with your ears.

- Breathe out to lower your shoulder blades down your back. Activate your core by engaging your pelvic floor, and draw your front ribs in towards one another.

- Press down into the Earth for steadiness, draw your inner thighs towards the midline of your body, then lift through the side waists.

- With each inhalation, lean back a little, imagining your spine easefully resting against the smooth curve of a crescent moon behind you.

- With each exhalation, imagine your loving heart opening toward the rays of a sun ahead of you.

Invite Love in.

ACCEPTANCE

When life is going well, it's easy to be accepting.
However, when we feel challenged, our ability to
let things be gets truly tested.

During these times, we tend to fixate on what's *not* going
well, and we resist the feelings that ARE here.
All we know is that we long for things to be different.

With time though, things WILL be different.

Everything changes.

The situation you're feeling challenged by *will* change ...

The way you're feeling right now *will* change ...

We can more readily accept the present moment
when we remember that nothing stays the same.

Acceptance is about allowing everything to be
exactly as it is – in *this* moment.

Even the difficult things.

How are you relating to challenging areas of your life?

*In this moment, can you accept that **it is what it is**
without needing to fix anything?*

When we embrace life exactly as it is right now – including
our own emotional response to what's going on,
we become more compassionate.

With *willingness* and *compassion* we surrender
to all that exists in the present moment –
whether it feels pleasant or unpleasant.

NOW is where all possibilities exist —
even those you have not yet awakened to.

✶

EMBODYING ACCEPTANCE

Gomukhasana
COW FACE POSE

Cow Face Pose is challenging for most, quickly giving rise to unpleasant sensations. It's what makes this pose so perfect for practising Acceptance. Breathe into all the moments – the pleasant and the unpleasant. This too shall pass.

✴ This is an invitation for you to allow Acceptance in your body.

- Place your hands and knees on the ground.

- Cross your right knee over the left, and slowly land your sit bones on the ground. You may wish to place a cushion or block underneath your bottom to help level the hips and lengthen the spine.

- Position your feet to the outer edge of the hips, pressing down through the last two toes of each foot.

- Breathe in, raising your right arm towards the sky. Keep your left arm lowered.

- Now bend both elbows, and aim to connect the fingertips of both hands behind your back. If they don't connect, take hold of your clothing or use a strap to grip onto.

- Breathe in to lift your sternum, keeping your heart space open. Breathe out and activate the core by drawing your lower front ribs in toward one another, and engaging the pelvic floor.

- Draw your chin in towards your throat, lift through the crown of your head, and edge your right elbow towards the sky, left elbow down towards the Earth.

Invite Acceptance in.

FORGIVENESS

If we had control over the design of our life,
there would be many events and situations
we would prefer not to experience.

Adversity happens in a moment of time. Yet it's common for
us to carry the weight of suffering for weeks, months, years
– even lifetimes beyond the event. It's a paradox to willingly
hold onto the memories that we feel most resistant to.

We don't want to carry them, but we do.
We don't know how NOT to.

To be free of the burden of the past is to Forgive.

'FOR - GIVE'
= *to give*

Some of us may try to force forgiveness by attempting to
think our way through it, bypassing or overriding
core **emotional wounding.** But that's not true Forgiveness.
Forgiveness is not a mental or 'will-full' process.

Forgiveness is an emotional movement
that happens in the heart as an automatic response,
once the emotion has been released.

How can we deal with emotions of the past?

IDENTIFY THE EMOTION.
Is it Anger, Fear, Sadness or Shame?

BE WITH THE EMOTION
How does it present in your body, breath and thoughts?
What does the emotion *feel* like?
Once you can feel the emotion, hold yourself gently.
The act was not okay, but the emotion is.

ALLOW
Honour the emotion by giving it time and space to release.

NOTICE
Acknowledge the space you've now created in your soul.
Where burdens once lay, sense and feel the space within,
through which divine love and grace can enter.
Now there is nothing left to forgive – the process is
complete. With wisdom in your heart from the experience
of the burden, new life choices can now be made.

GIVE THANKS
Now that you've resolved the emotion and integrated
the event, express Gratitude for the whole experience
and for the *growth* that it has brought your soul.

Forgiveness is liberation,
marking the milestones of our soul's maturity.

EMBODYING FORGIVENESS

Supta Baddha Konasana
RECLINING BOUND ANGLE POSE

Reclining Bound Angle Pose invites us to soften
our entire front body, allowing burdens to be released and
inviting in present-day liberation.

※ This is an invitation for you to allow Forgiveness in your body.

- Lie on your back, bringing the soles of your feet together and allowing the knees to drop away from one another (you may wish to place a cushion under each knee).

- Inhale, sweeping your arms above your head ...

- Exhale, allow the elbows to bend and arms to relax. You may wish to cup the elbows with the hands.

- Now, all you need to do now is *allow:*

    Allow the breath in ...

    Allow long, letting-go sighs out through an open mouth ...

    Allow your body to realise where holding-on exists ...

    Allow your body to give up any unnecessary tension, allowing for the release of burdens of the past.

    Invite Forgiveness in.

CLARITY

With Clarity, we see things clearly – without distortion.

A river can be so clear that it's possible to see straight through it. However, if there is an imbalance in the system, the waters can become murky.

Within YOU exists your own network of river-like channels known as 'nadis'. This network carries *prana* – vital life force, flowing through the 72,000 nadis that exist in your body.

If you're lacking Clarity, it's likely there's an obstacle in this energetic network. Your physical body may feel tired and sluggish. On a mental level, you may feel confused, foggy, and indecisive. Emotions may be heightened.

This is a time for inner *purification*.

When prana flows freely through your inner landscape, Clarity awakens.

Just as rain washes into the river network, you can use your *breath* to flood the nadis – shifting disturbances, dissolving obstacles and detoxifying your whole energetic network.

Breathe with an intent to connect your mind to your physical body and allow any obstacles in between to dissolve.

Now Clarity can lead the way.

EMBODYING CLARITY

Nadi Shodhana
ALTERNATE NOSTRIL BREATH

The pranayama practice of Alternate Nostril Breath
purifies and balances the nadis,
supporting Clarity to flow through you.

✳ This is an invitation for you to reveal Clarity in your body.

- Sit comfortably with your legs crossed, ensuring your hips are positioned a little higher than your knees (use a cushion to sit on if necessary).

- Place the back of your left hand on the left knee in Gyan Mudra. Connect your thumb and forefinger, while extending the last three fingers long.

- Bring your right hand in front of your face, anchor the pads of your index and middle fingers on the space between the eyebrows. This is the embodied seat of insight – the Ajna chakra.

- Close the right nostril with the thumb, then breathe in steadily through the open left nostril.

- Then, close the left nostril with the fourth and last fingers, and open the right nostril to breathe out.

- Breathe in through the open right nostril …

- Swap over, breathing out through the left nostril.

- Continue in this pattern for at least ten full rounds. Once complete, release the right hand down, and take a few easy breaths through both nostrils.

Invite Clarity in.

PLAY

The practice of yoga takes us on a journey to *enlightenment.*

'In-light-in-meant'
= Meant to be in the light

When our light is on, we see clearly – we see the truth.
That is, we perceive reality without distortion.

As we become illuminated in consciousness,
we also become equally aware of our own shadow.

Shadows can show up as mental, emotional,
energetic and physical distortions,
and are usually not pleasant to deal with.

It's understandable that it's hard to turn and face your
shadow, along the journey toward the light.

However, it's within our shadow that we can discover the
biggest opportunities for our own soul growth.

We need to get comfortable with the light
as much as the dark.

Play is what allows us to dance
between the polarities of light and dark.

To Play is to be curious, child-like and unafraid.

Being playful allows us to lean into our darker aspects, with
an attitude of creativity, growth and possibility.

Our shadow side is often judged to be a negative thing.
Yet it's only the judgement that constricts and confines
playful energy – not the shadow itself.

A playful attitude will illuminate both aspects of you equally
– without judgement, keeping you in flow state as you
balance the duality of your humanness.

Embrace your shadow
as much as your enlightenment.

EMBODYING PLAY

Camatkarasana
WILD THING

Wild Thing is a fun, yet advanced yoga pose. Honour any physical limitations with just as much playfulness as you would honour experiences of lightness and freedom.

※ **This is an invitation for you to initiate Play in your body.**

- From Downward Facing Dog (see page 57), raise your left leg up, bend through the left knee, and send the heel toward your bottom.

- Restabilise your shoulders by leveling them with one another, drawing the shoulder blades down the back, and hollowing out the armpits.

- Press both palms firmly into the ground, fingers spread wide. Keep the gaze up towards the navel.

- Slowly and gradually send your left foot behind you until the foot lands on the ground. Your left arm can reach up towards the sky, or behind you.

- For maximum stability, land your bottom down on the ground to reactivate the supporting muscles around your right shoulder. Press your right palm firmly into the ground, then, squeeze your glute muscles to support you to lift up into the backbend again.

- Breathe into your wide-open heart and smile!

Invite Play in.

CONNECTION

Deep down, we all long to end the feeling of separation.

Connection gives us a *sense of purpose*
and reason to BE here in this life – to exist.

Sometimes, we forget about the points of Connection that *already* exist for us. We fall into the trap of believing that we need to accomplish grandiose things, *do* more and *be* more, to feel a greater sense of Connection in life.

Relying on something *outside* of us, for an experience of Connection *inside* of us, is guaranteed to leave us feeling more disconnected than ever.

We need to *ground* Connection within us.

This body that you've been granted is only here temporarily.
The driver – your soul, is everlasting.

Your body is here to land Heaven on Earth.

Your physical body is the vehicle
for grounding divine Connection.

Remember and *honour* the points of Connection
that are already here.

Remember where you come from.

We are all living and breathing life through our bodies,
on this same planet Earth that we inhabit.
We are all made up of the same minerals found in the Earth
below us and the stars above us.
We are a product of the creation of our ancestors.
We are all connected through the simple fact that we *exist*.

*Remember where you are,
and what's right here now.*

Feel the Earth beneath your feet.
Feel the breath of life moving through your body.
Feel your heart beating.
Connect to what's here right now.

The more we honour Connection
that already exists, the more our
experience of Connection will grow.

EMBODYING CONNECTION

Savasana
CORPSE POSE

In Corpse Pose, keep your body still as if it were a corpse,
allowing for a deeper experience of being alive.
Honour the Connection that exists in this moment.

✴ This is an invitation for you to ground Connection in your body.

- With your back flat on the ground, extend your legs out long, and allow the lower back and hips to rest with ease (a cushion under your knees may be helpful).

- Extend your arms out alongside your body, palms open.

- Keep your chin drawn in toward the throat, offering space around the crown of the head.

- Spend time here focusing on the *felt* sensations of the breath in the *whole* body.

    Notice how the inhale feels in your whole body …

    Notice how the exhale feels in your whole body …

- See how your body and your breath are so connected, dancing with one another as they expand together, and surrender together.

- Feel the effects that this Connection of body and breath has on your *whole state of being.*

Invite Connection in.

POWER

Power is energy.

It moves through our body like electricity moving through a conduit, lighting up our *free will* and giving us the ability to *choose* our actions.

However, if Power is ungrounded the energy can get expressed as fear and anxiety. As we lose touch with Power, we feel like we're losing control.

We might even say, 'I feel powerless'.

If our behaviours and actions are motivated by fear, they can be harmful – even destructive. as we attempt to regain control *over* something – a*nything*, in order to feel Power again.

It's this misunderstanding of Power that keeps us stuck in an egoic cycle of self-preservation. The seductive ways of Power can tempt the human soul into unloving actions, which can play out as judgement, violence, attachment, corruption or manipulation.

What we need to do when we feel the surge of Power moving through us, is to **ground it.** From a grounded place, we can choose where to direct Power - we can *choose our response.* Now we can act on Power consciously – with love.

Divine Power is love in action.

EMBODYING POWER

Utthita Tadasana
FIVE-POINTED STAR POSE

In Five-Pointed Star Pose, we align from the ground up,
then radiate Power from the centre out.

✴ This is an invitation for you to activate Power in your body.

- From a standing position step your feet wide apart, toes pointing forwards.

- Extend your arms out to the sides, palms facing down.

- Breathe in, and feel your side waists lengthening.

- Breathe out, directing energy from your core all the way down through your legs and feet, into the Earth. Keep a microbend through both knees, to support you to remain firmly grounded.

- On your next breath in, allow just as much powerful energy to move from your core, up your body and out through the crown of your head. Keep your shoulders drawn away from your ears, and chin drawn in toward the throat.

- Build more stability now through your core (your physical Power-house). Engage your pelvic floor, draw your navel in toward the spine, and hug your front lower ribs in toward one another. Remain open across the heartspace.

- Rest your awareness on the meeting point of your lower ribs now. Your solar plexus chakra resides here - the energetic home of free will and personal Power.

Invite Power in.

TRUST

When we Trust, we feel safe.

When we feel safe Trust comes naturally, like a deep whisper that says, *'Everything's going to be okay'.*

It's hard to hear the whisper of Trust if *fear* is speaking the loudest. Fear creates uncertainty. When we're in the thick of it, we're not so sure that everything's going to be okay.

What we need to invoke is *certainty*.

If you don't have the intention that everything will be okay, then it probably won't feel okay.

Trust is the dart that flies through the air toward the dartboard of our heart's desires.

The two wings of Trust are *patience and divine timing*.

With Trust and Patience, you *allow* things to unfold in divine timing.

With Trust and divine timing, you offer *space* for your intent and desired outcome to merge.

As it is right now, everything is perfect – as long as you have Trust.

EMBODYING TRUST

Ustrasana
CAMEL POSE

Camel Pose requires a breath-by-breath approach
as we allow any guarding of the heart to dissolve.
Stay steady in your breath to keep rising
energies in motion – 'e-motions', moving through you.

> ☼ **This is an invitation for you to cultivate Trust in your body.**

- From a kneeling position, stack your knees, hips and shoulders in one long upright line.

- Draw your chin in toward the throat, lifting through the crown of your head.

- Take both palms to your lower back, with the elbows pointing behind you. Activate your pelvic floor.

- Breathe in and lift through the sternum. Breathe out to edge the fronts of your hips a little further forward as you come into the backbend.

- Keep doing this – lifting the heartspace on the inhale, then sending the hips forward again on the exhale. This will support you to cultivate Trust as you deepen the backbend – breath-by-breath.

- You may wish to land your palms down onto your heels. Ensure your hips stay stacked over the knees. Choose whether to tuck or untuck the toes, to suit the degree of your backbend.

Invite Trust in.

RECEPTIVITY

In today's society, success is commonly measured
by how much we achieve and accomplish.
It's a masculine paradigm.

Often, our first point of connection with each other is
based on 'what we *do*'. No wonder we've come to be
human *doings* rather than human *beings!*

If we take action ALL the time – without pausing to
rest and receive, warning signs start appearing:

Depletion of body, energy and mind ...
Exhaustion ...
Loss of inspiration ...

The light of our spirit dims.

It may seem like we're not receiving anything back,
for all the effort we're putting in. We may become resentful.

What's needed at this junction is *Receptivity.*

But how?

STOP
Press pause on the *doing*.

AWARENESS
Acknowledge to yourself that you're not receiving,
and you haven't been receiving.

INTENTION
Converse with your soul that you are now ready to *receive*.

Receptivity isn't a 'doing' word – it's an intent.
It's an invitation that invokes the feminine paradigm.

In truth, we're *made* to receive.
So why is it that we **block** our own Receptivity?

At a core level, are you feeling worthy?

Are your actions being driven by fear?
Fear of losing control? Or of losing your
sense of importance if you stopped all the 'doing'?

How can you start valuing yourself,
without having to DO anything?

Be still, and allow yourself to *feel*
the divine pulse of life in your body.

Give thanks for your very existence.

Notice what already is ...
Then you will receive.

EMBODYING RECEPTIVITY

Viparita Karani
LEGS UP THE WALL POSE

Legs Up the Wall Pose shows us how to stop, breathe and receive. The wall supports us to let go of any tension in our body, allowing us to feel the value of BE-ing here – without having to DO anything.

※ This is an invitation for you to allow Receptivity in your body.

- Find a wall to sit next to.

- Position yourself side-on to the wall, then lie down with your back to the ground.

- Now, spin around and allow your legs to rest up against the wall. Wriggle your bottom up close against the base of the wall.

- Allow your spine and head to rest easy on the ground.

- Place your arms out by your sides, with the palms of your hands open in a receptive gesture.

- Close your eyes and stay here for a while.

Invite Receptivity in.

COURAGE

Courage is like the flame of fire,
lighting up the path of truth.

The root of the word Courage is *cor* – the Latin word for *heart*. With Courage, we stand up for what's most important to our heart – our *core values*.

Our values are the coals that fuel the flame of Courage. They are the motivating force behind our decisions and actions in life.

However, if you don't know what your values are, there's nothing to stoke the flame of Courage. There's nothing to stand for.

Without Courage, fear breeds.
Uncertainty, doubt and confusion can destabilise our deepest convictions. Fear even has the power to completely stop us in our tracks, keeping us victim to current circumstances.

Fear dampens the fire of Courage.

The first step to reigniting Courage is to connect with your values. They've been with you since birth, and they guide you to *live with heart*.

There's nobody else on the planet who knows more about
your values than you do. Your values will be different to
those of another because they're uniquely yours.

Not everyone will agree with your values.
Yet there *will* be those who do align.

When we live by our own values,
we are connected internally to our soul.

With internal alignment,
life will bring external alignment.

With Courage, you light the way for a
soul-aligned, human life.

EMBODYING COURAGE

Utkata Konasana
GODDESS POSE

Activation of the core will support you to remain stable in Goddess Pose, giving you Courage to stand in your truth with an open heart – aligned with what matters most.

 This is an invitation for you to ignite Courage in your body.

- From a standing position, take the feet out wide.

- Bend your knees, turning the toes out at a 45-degree angle. Lower your sit bones down, adjusting the width of your feet if required.

- Now raise your arms up, bending the elbows at shoulder height, palms facing forward.

- Lower your shoulder blades down your back, and lift the crown of your head toward the sky.

- Inhale, pressing your hips forward and edging the knees back.

- Exhale as you activate your core. Engage the pelvic floor and draw the lower front ribs in toward one another.

- Ground down through the soles of your feet as you remain broad across the heartspace.

Invite Courage in.

PATIENCE

When we hurry through life,
there's no time to look around at what's here.

Hurrying creates a mind-body separation.
Our head is in a future moment yet our body is here,
in the *now*.

In an attempt to realign, the body strives to catch up with
where the head is at – the heart rate quickens and the breath
shortens. This makes us feel tense and anxious,
as though something is missing.

With Patience, nothing is missing.

Patience trusts that everything works in divine timing.
With Patience, we accept the present moment.

Longing, wanting and expecting things to be different from
how they are right now is what blocks Patience,
causing impatience.

If things don't turn out how we expect them to, we suffer
the loss of something that was never here in the first place.
It was just a thought.

Patience invites us to connect
with the gifts of what already is.

When we offer Patience, we're actually giving **love** and **space**.

Patience expresses *love* for *this* moment and *allows space* for *this* moment to unfold.

The consequence of our intention of Patience is that it returns *us* back to the present moment.

Thus, our Patience is a mirror:

'What I offer out, I receive within.'

Patience shows us the abundant magic of life that's already here in this moment – and reflects this abundance back to us.

EMBODYING PATIENCE

Ardha Chandrasana
HALF MOON POSE

Coming into Half Moon Pose requires Patience, so that you can honour all the moments that unfold along the way.

☼ **This is an invitation for you to invoke Patience in your body.**

- From a Warrior II Pose (see Sovereignty page 33) focus your gaze on a spot about a half metre ahead of your front foot.

- Begin leaning your weight into your front leg, hinging from the front hip, lowering your torso to the side. Place the fingertips of your front hand onto the Earth or on a block.

- Keep your gaze to the ground, as you push out through the heel of the raised foot, while also pressing down through the heel of your front foot.

- Keeping a microbend through the front knee, squeeze the glutes onto the hip bone. Now, turn the back foot skyward, externally rotating the back hip.

- Place your back hand on your hip, or extend the arm toward the sky, reaching out through the fingertips.

- Step-by-step, play with lifting your gaze to the side, then skyward, while maintaining balance.

Invite Patience in.

HUMILITY

So much of our growing years are spent *becoming someone*.
As we mould ourselves into our family, our broader
community and the world around us,
we develop an *identity*.

This is the ego – the part of our consciousness that needs
to know, with a fixed certainty, how the 'i' is positioned in
relation to the world around us.

While the ego is a normal human condition, important for
survival, it is also one of the greatest obstacles of Humility.

The ego has a motive of self-interest and self-preservation,
while Humility honours the *connection* of the Self to the
existence of *all*.

With Humility we relinquish control,
and *surrender* to the divine power of something greater.

Ego says, *'I am.'*
Humility says, *'I am still becoming.'*

Ego says, *'I am the expert.'*
Humility says, *'I am a student of life.'*

Ego says, *'I am the star.'*
Humility says, *'I bow to the stars.'*

Ego says, *'My way is best.'*
Humility says, *'I don't know.'*

Humility is okay with not knowing,
because the Creator knows.

With Humility, we yield to a higher source.

To be humble is to remember that we are in eternal *connection* and *co-creation* with something greater.

We are but a drop of water in the vastness
of the ocean of creation.

Call it life force, God, the Divine or Universe,
we are held by something greater

… we are part of something greater

… we are in union with something greater.

Bow to this remembrance.

EMBODYING HUMILITY

Uttana Shishosana
PUPPY POSE

Puppy Pose – also known as Heart-Melting Pose, shows us how to surrender the 'i' identity and reconnect our Self with something greater.

✨ This is an invitation for you to discover Humility in your body.

- Place your hands and knees on the ground.

- Ensure your knees are stacked directly under the hips. The toes are untucked, pointing straight back.

- Take a deep breath in, then breathe out as you walk your hands further forward. Allow your forehead to rest on the ground.

- Ensure the knees remain stacked under the hips. Adjust the positioning of your hands if needed.

- Engage the abdominals by hugging your front ribs in toward one another and activating the pelvic floor, to prevent collapsing through the lower back.

- With your palms flat on the ground and fingers spread wide, press down through your thumbs and index fingers to activate the entire length of your arms, and stabilise the shoulder joints.

- Broaden the collarbone, and lift your elbows away from the ground.

- Now, allow every exhale to soften and surrender the heart toward the Earth, as you invite Humility to wash over you.

Invite Humility in.

SERVICE

When life gets us down, one of the best things we can do is help someone else in need. But if we're wallowing in our own problems, *how could we possibly have energy to give to others?*

The act of selfless Service *(seva)* is the very thing that can pull us out from under the weight of our own human burdens, because our *spirit* branches out in consideration of others.

The act of seva is *unconditional* – giving without expecting anything in return. Yet, this way of giving aligns you with another human soul. *Connection* is a gift received by all as a result.

As we cultivate compassion for another, compassion envelopes our own soul.

As Mahatma Gandhi said,

'The best way to find yourself is to lose yourself in Service of others.'

Seva doesn't have to be grandiose. One small act is all that's needed to make a BIG difference.

Where in your life are you already in Service?

EMBODYING SERVICE

Matsyasana
FISH POSE

Fish Pose invites us to open our heart,
in a gesture of devotion.

☀ This is an invitation for you to initiate Service in your body.

- Lie flat on your back, and slide your hands underneath your bottom with the palms facing down.

- Begin to edge your elbows and shoulders under the back-body, and feel the chest naturally start to rise as though something is tugging your heartspace up.

- As you come into the backbend, your head will naturally lift away from the ground. If it feels ok for your neck, look behind you and allow the crown of the head to gently touch the Earth (avoid any pressing down).

- Continue grounding down through your elbows, sit bones and palms. Point your toes away from you.

- Breathe in through your nose. Then as you breathe out, open your mouth, devoting the exhalation to someone or something else in greater need.

Invite Service in.

BLISS

Bliss lives at the core of our being – our soul.

When we awaken to Bliss,
we reside in oneness with all that exists.
At the soul level, nothing is separate.

Bliss can be mistaken for an emotional moment of overwhelming joy, or a fleeting moment of happiness. Yet, it doesn't live in temporary moments, events and circumstances. Bliss isn't found in the 'right' job, other people, the perfect body, the new house or the next best thing.

Bliss is a state of being.

It's a constant, ever-pervading experience of
contentment and wellbeing.

When we tap into our own natural well of Bliss, we bring its essence into everything that we *do*, and everything that we *are*.

The source of Bliss lives beyond the physical, yet we can **feel** the resonance of Bliss at a cellular level.

Yoga teaches us that the physical body can be a starting point for examining how we are in relationship to everything in life – our inner world and the outer world.

As we bring movement to our body,
we see where obstacles to Bliss exist.

We quickly become aware if we are forcing, striving, judging or attaching. We see where we are undisciplined, unwilling and avoidant. It becomes clear where we could be more gentle, or where we could to sharpen our focus.

The way we move on the yoga mat is a reflection of how we move through life.

How you do one thing, is how you do everything.

We access Bliss once we have sifted through all the illusions of our human existence ...

and

It's our human existence that offers us the vehicle, through which we can *integrate* – and live in Bliss.

EMBODYING BLISS

Ananda Balasana
HAPPY BABY POSE

Happy Baby Pose creates flexibility and mobility through the
hips and hamstrings, while lengthening the spine.
Carry a sense of curiosity and playfulness with you,
and BE in Bliss.

☀ **This is an invitation for you to connect to Bliss in your body.**

- Lie on your back, with your feet flat on the ground, knees bent.

- Exhale, hugging your knees up into your chest.

- Now, reach your hands between the feet and wrap your fingers around the inner arches.

- Relax your head and shoulders back down on the ground. Flatten the spine toward the ground, including the back of the neck and the sacrum.

- Take your knees a little wider than your torso, edging them towards your armpits.

- Use your hands to pull your feet back towards you. With just as much effort, push the feet back into your hands.

- Bring lightness to the pose now, easing off any unnecessary tension and gently rolling across the spine and its supporting muscles.

Invite Bliss in.

KINDNESS

In a world of diversity and duality,
Kindness is a thread that *connects* us all.

It's a common language that all humans understand – across
borders, countries, cultures, ages, sexes and religions.
Kindness is *felt* in its expression,
without even having to speak a word.

Where walls of tension and judgement have been built,
Kindness even accepts that this is ok.

Instead of forcing anything to be different, fighting or fleeing,
Kindness oozes its warm nectar across tough exteriors,
inviting us to lean into difficulties and challenges
with more *tenderness*.

Kindness awakens the heart,
and is the goodness that exists within us all.

EMBODYING KINDNESS

Paschimottanasana
SEATED FORWARD BEND

Seated Forward Bend invites us to come into deep spinal
flexion, gently releasing tension across the whole back body.
Gather some blankets and cushions,
so you can support your body to melt.

✹ This is an invitation for you to remember Kindness within you.

- From a seated position, extend both legs out in front of you.

- Use your hands to shift the flesh of your buttocks away from your sit bones, grounding down through your seat. You may wish to prop your sit bones up on a cushion to support a long and integrous spine.

- Activate your legs by pushing out through your heels, drawing your toes back towards your body. Press the backs of your heels down into the Earth.

- Inhale to lift the arms up, lengthening through the side waists.

- Exhale to hinge forward from the hips. Allow the hands to land down wherever they've arrived along the length of your legs.

- With each inhalation, lift and lengthen the torso, straightening the spine. With each exhalation, surrender the front body more deeply towards the legs.

- If there's a lot of space between your legs and torso, insert a blanket or cushion (or three!) in the space. Allow your whole front-body to melt into the support that's before you.

Invite Kindness in.

CURIOSITY

Through the eyes of a clear-seeing soul,
the world is full of things to be in awe about.

To be Curious is to *remember* that life is an
experience of new and ever-changing moments.

When you awaken Curiosity, it's like saying,
'I wonder?'

However, along the ride of being a human, our natural
sense of Curiosity can give way to fixed perceptions.
We create judgements based on our interpretation of our
experiences, and the influence of those closest to us.
We assume this is how things are, how we are,
how others are, and how the world is.

Our perceptions define our reality.

With firm perceptions, we become 'set in our ways',
– a mind as fixed as concrete.

Yet, a perception is just *one* way of seeing things.
There are many possible ways to perceive life.

Without Curiosity, our experience of life become limited.

'In the beginner's mind there are many possibilities, but in the expert's there are few.'
– Shunryu Suzuki

Curiosity dissolves concrete ways of the mind, and delivers a warm, 'wonder-full' nectar that melts the edges of any pre-defined reality.

With Curiosity, the mind has the potential to open to an infinite field of possibility.

EMBODYING CURIOSITY

Salamba Bhujangasana
SPHINX POSE

Sphinx Pose asks that we open our heart
and gaze at what's before us – with Curiosity.

※ This is an invitation for you to awaken Curiosity in your body.

- Lie down, with the front of your body flat on the ground – face down, toes untucked.

- Place your forearms on the ground, stacking the elbows directly underneath the shoulders. Your chest will naturally lift away from the ground.

- Press down firmly through the elbows, forearms, and palms of the hands. Ensure all fingers are splayed wide.

- Lengthen through the legs, press the pubic bone down and engage the quadriceps. Point your toes and press the tops of the feet into the Earth.

- Continue to deepen your connection points with the Earth, as you rise up through the crown of the head and broaden across the heartspace.

- Set your drishti (a focused, yet effortless eye gaze) and back it with the intent of Curiosity.

Invite Curiosity in.

PEACE

Peace is a natural state of being.

However, it's hard to feel peaceful when there's chaos around us and storms brewing within.

We're wired to look outside of ourselves first, for causes of our own internal disharmony – it's an inbuilt mechanism.

We can fall into the trap of blaming what's happening in politics, families, and society, for the way we feel.

Disharmony exists as both an internal *and* external experience. Yet one does not govern the other.

When you become consciously aware that disharmony exists within you, the potential awakens for you to navigate yourself back to Peace.

Disharmony now becomes a *voice* that tells you something is out of alignment.

You are always the master of what goes on inside your own head and heart.

Ask yourself:

What needs to happen now in order to create alignment?

What needs to be let go of?

What needs to be spoken to?

Peace is revealed once you *choose* Peace.

It doesn't live 'out there' or at a future time when everything lines up the way you *think* it should.

Peace already resides *within* you, waiting patiently to be *unveiled*. The clarity of Peace never goes away. Like the sky, it only gets temporarily clouded.

All you need to do for Peace to shine through, is to *release your grip* on expecting anything to be different, from exactly how it is right now.

Being peaceful doesn't mean that you don't take action.
Instead, your actions are born from a place of Peace.

Peace is eternal.

EMBODYING PEACE

Anjali Mudra
SALUTATION SEAL

With the hands in Anjali Mudra, we honour life inside of us
and all around us – making Peace with life exactly as it is.

✷ This is an invitation for you to return to Peace in your body.

- Take a cross-legged seat, ensuring that your hips are level with, or higher, than your knees. Sit on a cushion if necessary.

- Use your hands to shift the flesh of your buttocks away from your sit bones, to attain a solid grounding through your seat.

- Breathe in as you lift and lengthen through your side waists. Breathe out to relax your shoulders away from your ears.

- Keep your chin drawn in toward your throat, lifting the crown of your head toward the sky.

- Bring the palms of your hands into a prayer-like position - Anjali Mudra, a gesture of honour.

- Bow your forehead slightly toward your fingertips, with reverence to this moment of life.

Invite Peace in.

REFLECTION

Life has a way of presenting **experiences** that *test us.*
These tests come in various packages, such as other people and undesirable events.

Sometimes the tests feel *extremely* unfair and unjust.
They might tip our world upside down. These experiences might be so impactful that it's hard to see how life could ever improve again.

However, these challenging life events are actually *gifts* – **IF** you choose to see them this way.

While there's nothing you can do to change the events of the past, what you **CAN** do is *heal* the past.

The suffering you have endured is longing to be lifted.
The time to release the power you've been giving to the past is **NOW**.

Ask yourself gently:

What learnings and gifts have I received?

*Because of the events of the past,
who have I now become?*

*What can I now offer the world based on my experience,
wisdom and authenticity?*

A prayer:

The events of the past have made me
who I am today.
They have shaped my soul.
Be it for better or worse, is up to me.
God has given me the gift of free will,
and for that I'm thankful.
With gratitude, I understand that
I am no longer victim to the past.

✺

EMBODYING REFLECTION

Supta Matsyendrasana
SUPINE TWIST

As you gaze 'behind you' in Supine Twist, remember,
everything has been pointing you towards
your own spiritual evolution. Emphasise your exhales and
allow the past to BE.

※ This is an invitation for you to bring Reflection in your body.

- Lie on your back with your feet on the ground, knees bent.

- Press down through both feet, lift your hips up and reposition them a little to the left.

- Now, hug your left knee into your chest and fully lengthen your right leg along the ground.

- Hold your left knee with your right hand, and breathe out as you send the knee across the midline of your body, coming into a closed twist.

- Extend the left arm out and look across it. You may wish to close your eyes.

- Ensure both shoulder blades connect to the ground. This may mean adjusting your left knee so it hovers or rests on something, like a cushion.

- Now that you're in position, rest the awareness on the breath, supporting you to deepen into the twist. Release your exhales through an open mouth.

Invite Reflection in.

GIVING THANKS

Lucia and Sasha, for your practice of Patience
while your mother devoted time to this book.

Melanie Spears, for mentoring me along this creative journey
from inception to completion. Your friendship is treasured.

Keturah Tracey, for bringing through such divine illustrations.

Danielle Mondhal, for your Sanskrit guidance.

Benay Dyor, Michelle Adams, Cindy Scott and Ashton Wood,
for 'soul-testing' my writings.

Stephanie Crane of Sleepy Hollow Creative, for your graphic
design skills that weaved everything together so beautifully.

Lee Buchanan, for enhancing Clarity with your editing touches.

Ping and the team at Everbest Printing.

The Mindful Yoga School community – teachers, trainees and
students, for showing me the power of intention embodiment.

My divine guides and teachers.

Most importantly, giving thanks to YOU – the reader,
for accepting this invitation of mine.

Together, may we demonstrate how to live
with big intention, for the benefit of all.

THE CREATOR & AUTHOR
Erin Lee

Erin Lee is a yoga, mindfulness and meditation teacher
based on the Sunshine Coast, Australia.

She founded The Mindful Yoga School in 2020
and leads yoga teacher training, meditation and mindfulness
teacher training programs, as well as other classes
and events, with the intention to expand
Presence, Courage and Compassion.

Erin's inspiration to create *The Little Book of Big Intentions*
landed after many years of sharing intention embodiment
in her mindful yoga classes.

While Erin was working with artist Keturah Tracey, the idea
was born to create guidance cards to support this book –
a wonderful testament to the co-creative magic available
to us all when we are in soul alignment.

THE ARTIST
Keturah Tracey

Keturah is an Australian-born artist. While working on the artwork in this book she was based in Austria feeding her gypsy spirit with new adventures, inspiration and joy.

Inspiration for Keturah's artwork comes from places she has travelled to, particularly India, which aroused her senses and captured her heart.

Keturah uses pastels to investigate the human form in her work, with a strong focus on the sacred feminine.

Through the use of form and colour she hopes to inspire and uplift your soul.

keturahartdesigns.com

the **mindful yoga** school

'Through our own demonstration of presence, courage and compassion, we show others how to do the same.'

Join Erin Lee for online video guidance
for embodying each intention:

themindfulyogaschool.com/bigintentions

INDEX OF YOGA POSES & INTENTIONS

Intention	Pose (English)	Pose (Sanskrit)	Page
Truth	Mountain Pose	Tadasana	9
Compassion	Easy Pose	Sukhasana	15
Balance	Tree Pose	Vrksasana	19
Grace	Dancer's Pose	Natarajasana	25
Sovereignty	Warrior II Pose	Virabhadrasana II	29
Gratitude	Bridge Pose	Setu Bandhasana	35
Surrender	Child's Pose	Balasana	41
Presence	Staff Pose	Dandasana	47
Wisdom	Downward Facing Dog	Adho Mukha Svanasana	53
Love	Crescent Moon Pose	Anjaneyasana	59
Acceptance	Cow Face Pose	Gomukhasana	65
Forgiveness	Reclining Bound Angle Pose	Supta Baddha Konasana	71

Intention	Pose (English)	Pose (Sanskrit)	Page
Clarity	Alternate Nostril Breath	Nadi Shodhana	77
Play	Wild Thing	Camatkarasana	81
Connection	Corpse Pose	Savasana	87
Power	Five-Pointed Star Pose	Utthita Tadasana	93
Trust	Camel Pose	Ustrasana	97
Receptivity	Legs Up the Wall Pose	Viparita Karani	101
Courage	Goddess Pose	Utkata Konasona	107
Patience	Half Moon Pose	Ardha Chandrasana	113
Humility	Puppy Pose	Uttana Shishosana	119
Service	Fish Pose	Matsyasana	125
Bliss	Happy Baby Pose	Ananda Balasana	129
Kindness	Seated Forward Bend	Paschimottanasana	135
Curiosity	Sphinx Pose	Salamba Bhujangasana	139
Peace	Salutation Seal	Anjali Mudra	145
Reflection	Supine Twist	Supta Matsyendrasana	151

THE LITTLE BOOK OF BIG INTENTIONS:
Guidance for embodied, purposeful living

Copyright © 2022 Erin Lee
Artwork Copyright © Keturah Tracey

This book is self-published by Erin Lee
themindfulyogaschool.com/bigintentions
with the beautiful support of Melanie Spears
and Giving Thanks Publishing
givingthanks.com.au

All rights reserved. Other than for personal use and where the owner of the work is quoted, no part of these cards or this book may be reproduced, stored in a retrieval system, or transmitted in any form or by any means without the prior written consent of the copyright holder, nor be otherwise circulated in any form of binding or cover other than that in which it was published and without a similar condition being imposed on the subsequent purchaser.

This book is intended to offer general wellbeing and yoga guidance. It is not intended to replace any other physical or mental health treatment or therapy. In applying guidance from this book, you are taking full responsibility for everything you act upon.

Printed by Everbest Printing Investment Limited.

ISBN: 978-0-646-85488-5